GO FACTS Physical science

Forces

A & C BLACK • LONDON

Forces

© 2007 Blake Publishing
Additional Material © A & C Black Publishers Ltd 2008

First published in 2007 in Australia by Blake Education Pty Ltd.

This edition published 2008 in the United Kingdom by
A & C Black Publishers Ltd, 38 Soho Square, London W1D 3HB.

Hardback edition
ISBN 9781408102633

Paperback edition
ISBN 9781408104866

A CIP record for this book is available from the British Library.

Author: Ian Rohr
Publishers: Katy Pike
Editor: Mark Stafford
Design and layout by The Modern Art Production Group

Image credits: cover (bottom) Shutterstock, p7 (top) Shutterstock, p11 (bottom)–
NASA, scanned by Kipp Teague; p14, (bottom), p15 (top)–Mark Stafford; p19
(top)–NASA Visible Earth; p21 (top)–NASA.

Printed in China by WKT Company Ltd.

This book is produced using paper that is made from wood grown in
managed sustainable forests. It is natural, renewable and recyclable.
The logging and manufacturing processes conform to the environmental
regulations of the country of origin.

contents

What are Forces?

A force is a push or pull that changes the speed, direction or shape of something.

Forces happen when **energy** is used. We see the combination of forces and energy acting all around us.

When you use energy to throw a tennis ball, you produce a force that causes it to move. When you catch a ball, you produce a force to stop it moving.

If you hit a tennis ball with a racquet, a force changes the ball's direction. If you squeeze the ball in your hand, a force changes its shape.

All objects are made of matter. The amount of matter an object contains is its **mass**. The more mass an object has, the more force needed to make it move, stop, or change direction or shape.

The muscles in your jaw produce biting and chewing forces.

A force can be strong, such as a tornado.

A force can be weak, such as the beat of a butterfly's wings.

A tug of war is two pulling forces on a rope.

pull

pull

5

Movement

An object remains still unless a force acts on it.

Objects resist movement. The force must be stronger than the object's **inertia** to make the object move. Inertia is how hard it is to move something.

Anything with mass has inertia. The more mass something has, the more inertia it has. This is why it takes a stronger force to move a bowling ball than a tennis ball.

Once something is moving, it keeps moving in the same direction as the force that caused it to move. It will only change direction if another force acts on it.

Anything that is moving has **momentum**. Momentum depends on the mass of an object and how fast it is moving. A fast moving car has more momentum than a slow one.

The batter hits a ball, which moves in the same direction as the force from the bat.

A real car and a toy car sit on the road. The real car has more mass than the toy car, and it needs a stronger push to make it move. The real car has more inertia.

Slowing Down

Once an object is moving, it keeps going unless another force makes it change direction or slows it down. The main force that slows things down is **friction**.

Friction happens when two surfaces rub against each other. Most surfaces are not perfectly smooth. Even a desk that looks smooth has little bumps all over it. If you slide a pencil case across a desk, the case rubs against it. This friction between the pencil case and the desk slows down the pencil case.

Friction creates heat. It can wear out objects that rub together. Many engine parts rub together. Oil in an engine reduces the effect of friction. This helps the engine last longer.

Friction is a contact force. This means objects need to be touching each other for friction to affect them. Some forces affect objects without touching them. These are called field forces. Gravity and magnetism are field forces.

Friction between the cards is helping to stop them from collapsing.

Rubbing your hands together produces heat from friction.

Even smooth objects have rough surfaces. This is a piece of wire viewed through a powerful microscope.

Friction is the force that slows down a rolling ball and eventually stops it.

Gravity

Gravity is a force between all objects. It pulls them towards each other.

Gravity is the force that pulls things towards the ground. Gravity pulls skydivers down when they jump from an aircraft.

The effect of gravity is called gravitational pull. Its strength depends on the mass of each object. You are attracted to the Earth because it has a much greater mass than you. The Earth's gravitational pull also keeps the Moon in **orbit** around the Earth.

The Sun's great mass means it has a powerful gravitational pull. It keeps the Earth, and the other planets in our Solar System, orbiting the Sun.

An object's **weight** is not the same as its mass. Mass is the amount of matter in an object, while weight is the force of gravity on it. An astronaut has the same mass on the Earth and the Moon. The astronaut weighs more on Earth because the Earth has a stronger gravitational pull than the Moon.

gravity

upwards force

To reach space, a rocket needs to produce an upwards force greater than the Earth's gravitational pull.

The Moon's gravitational pull causes tides on Earth.

GO FACT!

LONGEST

Captain Joseph W. Kittinger holds the record for the longest skydive. In 1960, he stepped from a balloon 25.8 kilometres above the ground. He fell for 4 minutes 37 seconds before opening his parachute.

There is six times less gravity on the Moon than on Earth. This means you can jump six times higher on the Moon than on Earth.

Magnetism

Magnetism is a force produced by magnets. Magnets are made of metal.

Magnets attract or **repel** other magnets. They are surrounded by invisible **field lines**. Field lines show the direction of the force.

Magnetism is strongest at the two ends of a magnet, which are called **poles**. There is a north pole and a south pole. A pole is attracted to the opposite pole of another magnet – north to south, and south to north. It is repelled by the same pole of another magnet.

The Earth acts like a giant magnet because of the metals inside it. The magnetic poles of the Earth are close to the North and South Poles. The field lines of the Earth start near the South Pole. They curve around in space and come together again near the North Pole. This is why a **compass** needle lines up from north to south.

An **electromagnet** is a magnet that runs on electricity. Its magnetic force depends on how much electricity flows through it.

Hikers, ships and planes use a compass to find their way. The compass needle always points to north.

TRAIL

Magnets that keep their magnetism are called permanent magnets.

DID YOU KNOW?
Monarch butterflies **navigate** using the Earth's magnetic field. They probably use small magnetic particles in their bodies as a built-in compass.

Powerful electromagnets are used to pick up scrap metal.

13

Make a Magnet

Follow the steps below to make your own magnet from a paperclip and see the effect of a magnet's field lines.

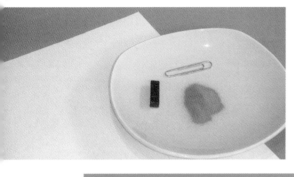

You will need:

- a bar magnet
- iron filings
- a paperclip
- a sheet of paper

1 Rub the paperclip along the magnet in one direction only. Do this about 15 times. This makes the paperclip magnetic.

2 Pick up some iron filings with the tip of the paperclip.

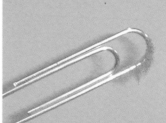

3 Lay the sheet of paper over the bar magnet. Sprinkle iron filings on the paper and tap the paper lightly to spread the filings. CAUTION: Handle iron filings with care.

If you have another bar magnet, try repeating step 3 with two magnets instead of one. The filings show the shape of the magnetic field. There are more filings at the poles of the bar magnet. This is where the magnetic force is strongest.

Moving in a Circle

You can tip a bucket of water upside down without the water falling out. How?

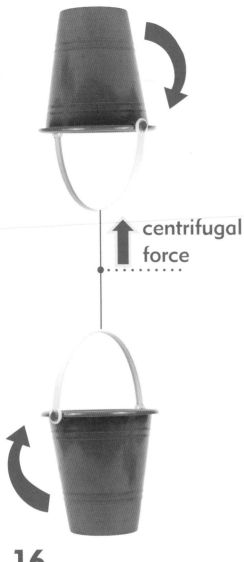

centrifugal force

Swing a bucket of water in a circle over your head. It feels as if the bucket wants to fly away. You can feel a force tugging on your arm. It is a force pointing away from the centre of the swinging. It is called a centrifugal force, which means a "centre fleeing" force.

The centrifugal force pushes the water to the bottom of the bucket, even if the bucket is upside down.

Swing it fast, and the water remains at the bottom of the bucket. The slower you swing, the less centrifugal force. At some point the water falls out.

You feel a centrifugal force when you go on a swing ride or around a corner in a car.

A satellite in orbit is pushed away from Earth by a centrifugal force.

17

Forces in the Planet

Forces cause earthquakes, wind and waves in and on the Earth.

The Earth's surface is made up of large, slow-moving plates of rock. The plates push against each other and pull apart. This releases energy, which causes the land above the plates to move. This might be an earth tremor that you can't feel or a violent earthquake.

Wind is caused by changes in **air pressure**. As the Sun warms the land, air above the land also warms. The warm air rises. This leaves behind an area of lower pressure. Cooler, heavier air rushes in to fill the space. This moving air is wind.

Ocean waves are caused by the force of the wind. As it blows, the wind pushes water ahead of it. The pushing force transfers energy from the air to the water, forming waves. The largest waves are made by strong winds acting over long distances.

THE TALLEST

The tallest wave measured was more than 27 metres high–taller than a nine-storey building. It was created by Hurricane Ivan (pictured), in the Gulf of Mexico in 2004.

The more energy an earthquake releases, the more force it has.

Wind farms use wind to generate electricity.

19

Forces All Around

Everything we do involves forces. Forces are at work whether you are playing basketball or flying in an aeroplane.

When a basketball player shoots, a push force sends the ball towards the net. Friction with the air slows the ball down. Gravity pulls it back towards the court. The ball would just keep going up without the action of these forces.

An aeroplane has four forces acting on it. The engines produce a forwards force, called thrust. The wings produce an upwards force, called lift. Friction from air rushing over the aeroplane, called drag, slows it down. Gravity pulls it towards Earth.

What happens to an object depends on the sum of all of the forces acting on it. The basketball reaches the net because the force of the shot is greater than the effects of gravity and friction. The aeroplane moves forwards because the thrust from the engines is greater than gravity and drag.

drag

gravity

thrust

lift

The movement of an object depends on the sum of all forces acting on it.

gravity

friction

push

Many animals are **streamlined** so that they can move through the water – and air! – with less drag.

21

Your Weight in Space

The stronger the gravitational pull of a place, the more you weigh there. Let's say you weigh 50 kilograms on Earth.

Standing on:		Your weight in kilograms:
Moon		8.3
Earth		50
Mars		18.8
Jupiter		118.2
Sun		1,353.6

Glossary

air pressure	the downwards pressure from the weight of the atmosphere
compass	a device for finding direction that uses the Earth's magnetic field
electromagnet	an iron device that becomes magnetic when electricity passes through it
energy	the power from something, such as oil, which can do work, such as providing heat
field lines	lines that show the direction of a magnetic field
friction	the force which makes it difficult to move against or through something
inertia	an object's tendency to remain still
mass	the amount of matter in an object
momentum	the force that keeps an object moving
navigate	to direct the way that something travels
orbit	the path along which objects move around a planet or star
poles	the ends of a magnet
repel	to force something to move away
streamlined	shaped to move quickly through liquid or gas
weight	the amount that something weighs; the force of gravity on its mass

Index